DEFEATING MENTAL ILLNESS

NICK GRIEMSMANN

WESTBOW
PRESS®
A DIVISION OF THOMAS NELSON
& ZONDERVAN

Scripture taken from the New King James Version®. Copyright © 1982
by Thomas Nelson. Used by permission. All rights reserved.

WestBow Press books may be ordered through booksellers or by contacting:

WestBow Press
A Division of Thomas Nelson & Zondervan
1663 Liberty Drive
Bloomington, IN 47403
www.westbowpress.com
1 (866) 928-1240

ISBN: 978-1-9736-2218-5 (sc)
ISBN: 978-1-9736-2217-8 (e)

Print information available on the last page.

WestBow Press rev. date: 03/19/2018

CONTENTS

FOREWORD

Millions of people struggle with mental illness. This book is specifically dedicated to those hurting individuals. My prayer is that this book helps you and / or someone you care about find relief from the torment of mental illness.

Please know that I, Nick Griemsmann, am not a professional counselor, psychiatrist, or any other medically trained person. I am just someone who cares and wants to try to help those affected by mental illness.

This book was written to inform the reader about my personal testimony of fully recovering from schizophrenia and to offer hope. The things written here are to try to help and not meant to judge or offend any individual or group of people. I deeply care and truly believe there is great hope for individuals to fully recover from any type of mental illness.

I wrote this from my heart to yours.

Sincerely,

Nick Griemsmann

This book is dedicated to every person who has been tormented by a mental illness. You are not forgotten.

Nashville Airport, Batons, and Hollywood

"It is incurable." said the psychiatrist to my mother and me. It was the fall of 2003 and we were sitting together in a county behavioral health clinic in Phoenix, Arizona. "Incurable?" my mother replied to the doctor.

The psychiatrist was in her early 70's, very depressed looking and staunch in her reply back to my mother, "Yes, paranoid schizophrenia is an incurable mental illness. Your son will always have to take the prescribed medications, collect (government) disability, either live with you or in a group home, most likely never be able to hold down a job and will definitely not be able to have his own family."

She went on to say, "And sometimes with these types of cases, after ten or so years the patient may go into a catatonic like state. Which is kind of like being what we would call - a vegetable."

My mother's mouth dropped open as she hopelessly looked over at me, her 23-year-old son who could barely speak because the voices had taken over almost his entire mind. She grabbed my hand and said, "Nick, it's going to be alright!"

The full effect of what the doctor told us that day didn't really hit me until a few weeks later. As I sat in my mother's home (that's where I was living at the time), suddenly, I realized that a medical professional had diagnosed me with an "incurable" mental illness

1

and that I was never (so I thought) going to get any better. My hopes and dreams for the future were crushed.

I believed that doctor's negative report for over six months, until one day, I decided to do something about it - fight back!

I was diagnosed with schizophrenia in my early twenties. To be exact, it was the week before my 23rd birthday. Like many kids, I grew up in a pretty normal non-religious household. I attended church a couple of times with my family, mostly on major holidays. Overall, I didn't know much about religion.

My parents ended up divorcing when I was eight years old. After the divorce, my Dad wasn't around that much. I learned a lot about being a man from watching television and from my older brother and his friends.

Fast forward to the late 90's - I ended up dropping out of high school in the 10th grade because of a bad marijuana and alcohol addiction. Basically, I partied way too much.

At 19 years old, I was a bartender and struggling trying to get through community college. When I was 21, a fancy nightclub opened down the street from where I was working and decided to apply for a position. The bar manager hired me, and honestly, I thought I was on my way to fulfilling my life's ultimate dream – bartending at one of the hottest nightclubs in Scottsdale, Arizona.

For that period in my life, I was mingling with rich people, dating beautiful women, partaking of all sorts of different illegal drugs, drinking heavily and at the same time completely miserable inside. I became unsatisfied with what I believed was going to satisfy me.

Working at the nightclub, my heart started to feel heavy about pouring drinks for people who I figured were probably going to drive home drunk. I also started feeling bad about being part of an environment where both men and women that I knew were married, would be looking to be intimate with people other than their own spouse. This made me start to regret my job.

With my heart heavy about nightclub bartending along with the feeling of conviction for my own personal sins it led me to start exploring God and the afterlife. I wondered about what would happen when I eventually died. Would I be judged for all the negative things that I had done and words that I had spoken in life? I truly needed answers.

I started occasionally watching religious broadcasts on television and then eventually purchased a Bible. I used to hide the Bible underneath my bathroom counter because I was afraid my roommates would think I was crazy for reading it.

As I read the Bible, I felt a heart tug towards Jesus. The problem was, I didn't know how to find a release from all the heart stuff and the heavy blanket of conviction that felt like was always sitting on my shoulders. I sincerely felt bad for my lifestyle and behaviors. I knew in my heart that I was not living a good life. I sincerely wondered if I was going to make heaven at the end of my life or not. I definitely didn't want to miss out on heaven, who would?

You may feel like that today. You may feel as if your lifestyle isn't right and maybe felt convicted in your heart about it. Let me tell you something wonderful – forgiveness is nearer then you think. Father God cares about you. In reality, Jesus is just a prayer away. Be encouraged to pray to Him daily.

One afternoon, I decided to call a Christian prayer line. The lady on the phone asked me, "Are you saved?" I didn't understand what she meant because there were so many different denominations and religions. In my mind, the term saved could mean a whole lot of things. I asked her what she thought it meant. She explained the Gospel and encouraged me to pray with her. She led me in a repentance prayer to God. I personally asked Jesus Christ to forgive me, save me, and wash me in His precious blood.

Honestly, at first, I was just saying the prayer because I felt like

I had to. The lady, to me, seemed kind of pushy. But looking back, I am so thankful for her because that prayer changed my entire life.

During the prayer, as I said the name of Jesus, I could feel this cleansing warm presence (now I know it was the Holy Spirit) rush over me and clean my entire soul. It was such an amazing feeling. I will never forget it.

On a sunny April day in 2002, I dedicated my life to God and was forgiven and saved for all eternity. With one simple prayer of faith, I was instantly delivered from desiring the party lifestyle, drinking, and drugs. I had received a new life, I was truly born again.

Therefore, if anyone is in Christ, he is a new creation; old things have passed away; behold, all things have become new. -2Corinthians 2:17

After having the wonderful spiritual experience, I tried to find a church to attend. I was browsing the Internet for Christian churches and happened to fall on a website for a man who claimed to be one of the final two witnesses mentioned in the Book of Revelation. Of course, he was not one of the two witnesses, but being a young convert to Christianity I did not realize there were false teachers. I took him at his word.

On this person's website, it said that his church provided all the things necessary for life (clothing, food, shelter, etc.) to all those who truly wanted to serve the Lord with all their heart, soul, mind, and strength. This seemed like a perfect place for someone like me who wanted to serve Jesus.

Without even thinking, I decided to move away from my family and friends and live at one of the church compounds to "serve the Lord". The compound where I ended up living was in Arkansas.

In Arkansas everything seemed okay at first. The place didn't seem like a cult. But now that I look back, there were some major red flags that warned me that I was in a cult. Unfortunately, I overlooked them. I was naïve, trusted people easily, and was relieved to be far away from my past drinking buddies. I felt so clean and free inside. I thought living in a commune was going to keep me safe from outside negative influences.

Within a month or so, the church leaders told me that my family was of the devil and that I was not to have any more phone contact with them. They said that occasionally I could send a letter or two, but that was pretty much it. By the time they told me this, I was already at a point of believing whatever they said. In my mind, I was serving the Lord in the one true church while being taught by one of the two final witnesses. I soon found out that I was greatly deceived.

At the church compound, whenever anyone would get in trouble for something, an example would be not doing chores, sleeping during church, getting in an argument with another member, etc., or someone reported you for doing something against the prophet's commands, the offender would get a cassette tape sent from the church office.

One time, I wore a pair of shorts in the church sanctuary. You should have seen how mad the church leaders were. One of them said that I was sinning against the Lord because the prophet had a rule that no one could wear shorts in the sanctuary. He told me that God could kill me right there and burn me in hell for not listening to the commands of the prophet. I was so scared!

Experiencing this type of condemnation moved me to fearfully obey whatever they told me where commands of the prophet. They could have told me anything and I would have obeyed them.

The rebuking cassettes were cassette tapes given to members that were filled with the leader yelling at the offender and threatening to kick them out of the church. I once saw a man get one of these tapes and he was shaking in horror. The leader was yelling at him, saying that he was going to burn in hell if he didn't repent and strictly follow all his commands. The poor man was so frightened and honestly, I was too.

Along with these rebuking cassettes, it was mandatory to go to church service every single night. During these redundant services, we would do three songs for worship, listen to short testimonies, have an older person in the church share from the Bible (usually about hell) and then they would play a teaching on cassette tape from the leader or watch conspiracy theory videos on a big television set.

When we did have to listen to the leader preach, it was almost always on hell fire and brimstone. I was literally in fear and torment every day. I had this vision of God in my mind, he was an old, mean, angry man sitting in the sky that was excited about burning everyone alive in hell. In my belief system, barely anyone made it in to heaven.

I never did see or meet the leader of the cult face-to-face. I only spoke briefly on the phone with him. He didn't live at the compound but was at a different location. The story goes that he was living with child brides.

I didn't know anything about the child brides until after he was arrested in 2009 when it was reported on national news. I left the cult in 2003. The leader was eventually convicted for his crimes and sentenced to 175 years in federal prison, where he eventually died.

After being in the cult for about five months, suffering from immense fear and tormented daily of the fear of hell, I started hearing voices in my mind. I first thought the voices were angels and the Holy Spirit.

One night while on a trip to go pass out thousands of pieces of literature to recruit more cult members, the voices took over. They told me to run off from the group. After walking miles and miles while talking out loud to voices in my head, I was found screaming inside the baggage claim area at the Nashville International Airport. Yes, you are reading a true story.

After leaving the group and walking around the city, I found myself in the morning sitting in a large grass field near the airport. I remember laying in the grass so afraid, because I had run off from the cult. I thought I would never be able to be saved again.

The false teacher taught us that we were in the one true church and that meant if we ever left, we left Jesus and the Holy Spirit. He told us if we deserted, we were going to be condemned to hell for all eternity because we would be considered blasphemers of the Holy Spirit.

Inside the airport, I went in the baggage claim area to get a drink of water and to use the restroom. Inside the restroom, the voices gave me an idea. They said that I needed to get on my knees in front of everyone, close my eyes, and start praying to God loud for everyone to hear. The voices told me if I did what they said, then God would supernaturally translate me to Ground Zero in New York City to preach to everyone. They told me that I was a great end-times prophet.

I walked in to the middle of the baggage claim and in front of 200+ people, I dropped to my knees, closed my eyes, and started screaming to God in prayer. That was until the airport police arrived - Thud! Pow! Ouch!

They yelled at me to stop, but I wouldn't. I was then hit by a police officer. I fell to the floor still screaming because I thought the louder I screamed, the faster God would translate me. After physically restraining me, the police then hog tied me and carried me out of the airport. What a wild scene that certainly was.

After trying to talk with me, the police officers noticed that I was extremely dehydrated and in need of mental health treatment. I ended up being transported to a mental hospital in Nashville for observation. I spent my 23rd birthday sitting in a mental hospital.

After the observation time, I was released and put on a bus back to Phoenix. Once home, my family could tell I had been brain-washed by the cult. All I could talk about was the Bible and hell. I couldn't hold a conversation. I could only tell people that they were going to go to hell unless they repented and joined the one true church in Arkansas. There was little my family could do for me.

Somehow, I ended up on a bus back to the cult after spending about one month with my family and taking medications for schizophrenia. This time, I went to the cult outpost outside Hollywood, California instead of the commune in Arkansas. I was embarrassed to go back to Arkansas with the people who knew me from before. I figured the California outpost would be better.

While I was at the compound in California, I didn't take the psychotropic medications that had been prescribed. This was because I didn't believe I really had a mental illness and the cult leaders said I was not allowed to take medications while living there.

About two weeks in California without the medications, I started having horrible hallucinations. Hearing even louder voices and doing some weird stuff. So weird, that one evening the church leaders told me to grab all my belongings and said to me, "You are going to go street preaching."

I quickly grabbed everything and jumped into the van excited to have the chance to tell people about joining the one true church. Instead of street preaching like they said I was going to go do, the men stopped off at a fast food restaurant. They walked me in and bought me a sub sandwich.

I put my head down to take a bite of the sandwich and they were gone. I was scared out of my mind. I thought I had blasphemed the Holy Spirit and had lost my salvation – again!

I walked outside to look for the church leaders, but I couldn't find a trace of them. The voices then came and started telling me that I had to close my eyes. They said if I opened my eyes up I would go immediately to hell. Of course, because of how afraid I was, I listened to the voices and did everything they told me to.

These experiences may sound silly to you but try to remember that I was a young man who really loved Jesus and wanted to serve Him with my whole heart. I sincerely thought God was speaking to me in my head and telling me to do things. I thought Jesus was testing my faith.

Not too much longer after leaving the fast food restaurant, I somehow fell asleep at a bus stop. The next morning, I woke up with the sunrise. All the fear gripped me again. I truly thought I lost my salvation. What was I to do? Where could I go? The church had kicked me out and it was the only one true church in the world. I felt doomed.

The voices came flooding in and said, "Jesus Christ is coming back to judge the world right now, look up and see." So, I looked up at the sun and it was coming through the clouds. At that moment I had a hallucination. In my mind I thought I saw Jesus riding a white horse coming to judge the world. Then the voices said, "You have to show the world that you are not ashamed." I said back to them, "I am not ashamed of Jesus, I love Him." Then the voices replied, "Then take off all of your clothes and show the world that you are not ashamed of Jesus."

So, yes, that's what I did. On a street corner in Hollywood, California in 2003, only six months after knowing Jesus as my Lord and Savior, I took off all my clothes in public and walked down the street completely naked. That was the most embarrassing experience of my life.

It seemed like I was only naked for a few seconds before an ambulance came and transported me to the hospital. They thought I was on heroine or some other heavy drug. After the emergency room doctors checked me out I was transported to yet another psyche hospital for observation.

I wrote these details down to let you know that I have dealt with some traumatic experiences and that there is hope for you and / or your loved ones, no matter how bad it may seem.

I used to have many scary hallucinations. At times, it seemed that the radio and television would talk directly to me. One time my neighbor's television set felt connected to my brain waves through the wall. It's hard to explain but was a very scary hallucination.

I had so much anxiety underneath my skin, in my stomach and mind that I couldn't even take my dog for a walk outside. I was scared every second of my life. I had a bad case of agoraphobia. All I could do was pace back and forth all day long in my mother's living room.

I even thought the President of the United States had me under surveillance. An alien type being appeared right next to me and talked to me. In fact, I had lots of different people talk to me that weren't even there. I had people who I thought were angels appear to me and some other weird things that most people would never believe. Yes, you could say I was in a pretty hopeless situation in my early twenties.

There are a lot of other things that I could tell you about with hallucinations and trips to and from over six different psychiatric facilities across four states (Tennessee, California, Arizona and Oklahoma), but this book is not about the hallucinations and mental hospital stays, this book is to encourage, uplift and give hope.

Amazingly, during and after the schizophrenia recovery, I worked in the behavioral health field. I used my story of recovery to help many mentally ill individuals. As an Administrator for a behavioral healthcare company, I used my experiences to impart knowledge and wisdom in the design of classes, groups and other things to help people in the community. I also was invited to speak at conferences and events to share my recovery story with others. I have been interviewed both on video and for articles written by people in the behavioral health field from different parts of the country.

I think it's amazing how God placed me in the same behavioral healthcare company that I used to be a patient of. I started off part-time helping in an events program to eventually running five different programs with 40+ employees underneath me, including counselors, and others that were way more credentialed then I was. My job was a miracle.

In writing this book, I'm not only coming from experience with my own personal struggles with mental illness but also incorporating my years of working in the behavioral health field and from my experience in Christian ministry to help empower you in your own recovery journey.

In the next few chapters, I am going to go over the below key points. God bless you as you continue to read on with an open heart and mind.

Key Points

- What is mental illness and where could it come from?
- Some steps that I took that could help you in your own personal recovery.
- How I believe that you can minister whole person freedom to yourself and others.
- Breaking the lies inside the mind.

What Would Jesus Do?

The term mental illness is a word many people use to describe someone who suffers from a disorder of the mind. Some of the terms you might have heard before are Bipolar Disorder, Clinical Depression, Paranoid Schizophrenia, Schizoaffective Disorder, Post Traumatic Stress Disorder (PTSD), Multiple Personality Disorder (MPD), Obsessive Compulsive Disorder (OCD), General Anxiety Disorder (GED), etc.

I personally believe most of these illnesses get their label from the symptoms the person manifests. For instance, if someone has a diagnosis of bipolar, it's usually because they go from a high-high in their personality and actions, to a low-low, hence the term bipolar. If someone has been diagnosed as having schizophrenia, it's usually because the person has somewhat of a distorted reality and suffers from visual and / or auditory hallucinations.

Most mental illness diagnoses are usually because of what the doctors say are chemical imbalances in the person's brain. Because of these chemical imbalances, doctors prescribe psychiatric medications to try to help stabilize or normalize the suffering individual.

Most in the medical field will tell you that mental illness is manageable, but not curable. Meaning, the same report my mother and I received at the behavioral health clinic about having no hope for full recovery is repeated over and over to families all over the world. This can leave people feeling completely hopeless.

One time, I was sharing my recovery story in a behavioral healthcare setting and after I finished, a psychiatrist raised her hand to what I believed was to ask a question. Instead, she seemed upset and told everyone in attendance that fully recovering from schizophrenia was impossible because it was an incurable mental illness. It seemed that she was trying to get me to argue with her. She kept saying that I must have been misdiagnosed and may never really had schizophrenia in the first place. I kindly let her know that I had hundreds of pages of medical documents indicating that may different doctors all diagnosed me the same thing. And of course, she didn't realize this one thing - I had Jesus on my side. He was my healer and deliverer. He healed me of mental illness and He can heal you too!

So, where does mental illness come from? I'm not a doctor or medical professional so I can't really answer that question in a medical sense, but I can try to answer it in a biblical sense.

This might be new and maybe a little scary for some of you, but out of love for people I want to share what I have found to be my truth. You can take it or leave it, that's between you and God.

In my own personal experience, I believe through trauma and accepting many lies in my mind, spiritual strongholds somehow attached to my soul (mind, will, and emotions) and caused a possible chemical imbalance which led to the eventual diagnosis of schizophrenia. The Bible mentions spiritual strongholds and the importance of renewing our minds.

For the weapons of our warfare are not carnal but mighty in God for pulling down strongholds, casting down arguments and every high thing that exalts itself against the knowledge of God, bringing every thought into captivity to the obedience of Christ, and being ready to punish all disobedience when your obedience is fulfilled. -2Corinthians 10:4-6

And do not be conformed to this world, but be transformed by the renewing of your mind, that you may prove what is that good and acceptable and perfect will of God. -Romans 12:2

This might be the first time you ever heard of mental illness possibly being caused by spiritual strongholds, but I believe this could be the case with many tormented individuals. I came to this conclusion through my own experience with mental illness and years working in behavioral health and Christian ministry.

I do want to say that I personally do not believe all mental illness cases are caused by spiritual forces. The human body is a very complex system and we can't blame everything on evil spirits.

When I was struggling with schizophrenia, my mother used to go on the Internet and search for resources to try to help me feel better. It seemed like every night she would sit on the computer looking at websites and reading articles about possible schizophrenia cures. She had me eating a lot of fish because it was supposed to help with my brain chemistry. I don't know if that really worked, but I do want to take a moment to thank my mother for being such a great supporter during the toughest time in my life. Thank you, mother, for being so strong and standing by me all those years. I love and appreciate you very much.

Through the years, I have talked with many people about mental illness. It seems to me that most believe that mental illness is caused solely by a chemical imbalance. Even a high percentage of Christians dismiss that spiritual strongholds could possibly be causing a chemical imbalance in an individual.

A stronghold to me is a place in someone's belief system that is built on lies. When we continue to believe lies then a stronghold can grow more fortified. I believe as it gets stronger, it can lead a person into making bad life choices, give them emotional / physical issues and even cause mental illness.

I think of a stronghold as a place in the soul (mind, will, and emotions) where evil spirits can try to mess with the entire person. They do this by continually lying to them and giving them false beliefs and emotions. Therefore, I believe knowing Jesus, the Truth, can set people free.

Today, I have something called a Letter of Decertification. I had to go through many doctors and clinical reviews to receive it. This letter states that I am no longer diagnosed with any type of mental illness.

"And you shall know the truth, and the truth shall make you free." -John 8:32

I used to ingest eight to ten psychotropic medications per day and go to a clinic to receive a medication shot in my hip / buttocks muscle every two weeks. It made me feel shameful to get the shot from the nurse. I hated it so much and sometimes cried about it.

But now, I can look back and be happy for what I went through because my experience may help you or someone you care about. Believe me, there is a light at the end of the tunnel!

You may be wondering about young children with mental illness, if they can have these strongholds too. It's my personal belief that young children can somehow be affected spiritually just like adults can be. But how can this be?

I believe it could be any number of reasons, including trauma in the womb, rejection, abuse, DNA transfer from parents, etc. There literally could be hundreds of other things as well. But I have found that looking at the positive is way more productive than focusing on the negative. Focus on God's word. There is hope for suffering children. The Bible tells us that Jesus didn't only heal adults, but children as well.

And when they had come to the multitude, a man came to Him, kneeling down to Him and saying, "Lord, have mercy on my son, for he is an epileptic and suffers severely; for he often falls into the fire and often into the water. So I brought him to Your disciples, but they could not cure him." Then Jesus answered and said, "O faithless and perverse generation, how long shall I be with you? How long shall I bear with you? Bring him here to Me." And Jesus rebuked the demon, and it came out of him; and the child was cured from that very hour. -Matthew 17:14-18

For a woman whose young daughter had an unclean spirit heard about Him, and she came and fell at His feet. The woman was a Greek, a Syro-Phoenician by birth, and she kept asking Him to cast the demon out of her daughter. But Jesus said to her, "Let the children be filled first, for it is not good to take the children's bread and throw it to the little dogs." And she answered and said to Him, "Yes, Lord, yet even the little dogs under the table eat from the children's crumbs." Then He said to her, "For this saying go your way; the demon has gone out of your daughter." And when she had come to her house, she found the demon gone out, and her daughter lying on the bed. -Mark 7:25-30

Many children nowadays struggle with anxiety, anger, fear and phobias. It's my personal belief that one major reason for this is because of a child's living environment. Did you know that children's minds are like vacuum cleaners and can take in everything that comes their way? This can be good and bad at the same time. Low self-esteem, depressive thoughts, rebellion, and fear type belief systems can be lodged into a child's mind easily, if exposed a lot to the wrong things. As they say, "Garbage in, garbage out."

The more trauma that happens, and garbage a child takes in, the more problems a child could end up with. Protect your children the best you can. The Holy Spirit can help you, if You sincerely ask Him to.

Please know that if someone has a child suffering with a mental illness, it does not mean they are a bad parent. Mental illness can be caused by many different things that are no one's fault. Sometimes it's one big mystery of specifically why a child is manifesting a physical, mental or emotional illness. Do not condemn yourself if your child has been diagnosed. Instead, trust God's promises for healing and wholeness. Jesus loves your child more than you do!

I have found that many mental illnesses in adults could be caused by abuse, trauma, alcohol and drug use, etc. Many soldiers get diagnosed with Post Traumatic Stress Disorder (PTSD) because of the horrific experiences during times of war. Mental illness can also manifest after experiencing spousal abuse, spiritual abuse, accidents, rape, and the list goes on.

Do you see a similarity with the things I've listed here and what the Bible refers to as sin?

For instance, a child is abused by a family member. This could somehow allow for spiritual strongholds to be built inside the child's soul (mind, will, and emotions) which could lead to the child experiencing torment. Along with the abuse, negative thoughts and emotions flood in. The lies and feelings can be anything from it's your fault, you're no good, you're not loved, no one likes you, you hate yourself, you should kill yourself, etc.

Do you see how a traumatic experience could allow lying thoughts and emotions to build and start to form a stronghold that in turn could lead to an emotional / mental illness?

I have also seen mental health issues rooted in childhood abuse not manifest until the person is an adult. Think of it this way; a seed planted can eventually grow to become a tree. In the same way an evil seed can grow up to become a big, evil tree (the tree representing mental, emotional, or physical illness later in life).

It takes a while for a seed to become a big tree, but it eventually does. Some seeds take a short time to grow and some take longer. And some seeds die out. Same way to think of how sin destroys people's lives. The seed of sin is planted and will either grow small, grow large or die out.

Then, when desire has conceived, it gives birth to sin; and sin, when it is full-grown, brings forth death. -James 1:15

The blood of Jesus cleanses us from all sin so that the negative seeds that we or others have planted in us can die.

But if we walk in the light as He is in the light, we have fellowship with one another, and the blood of Jesus Christ His Son cleanses us from all sin. -1John 1:7

So, like I mentioned earlier, a mental illness that manifests in an adult could be connected to something that happened many years ago when they were a child. Helping that person process through their past prayerfully, in love, forgiveness and grace could help that person receive true freedom.

Here's a couple more examples to help you - a soldier sees his friends die on the battlefield. Going through that type of trauma could allow a stronghold to be built in the soldier's soul. The soldier can't seem to shake the memories engrained inside his / her mind and the emotions of fear, anxiety, sadness, etc., overtake them to a point where they cannot function normally without psychotropic medication.

A person addicted to drugs could be destroying their body / brain and at the same time allow false beliefs to create strongholds of addiction. These strongholds continue to lie to the person, pulling them further down the path of destruction.

A wife that is verbally abused by her husband could start

suffering from depressive, negative thought patterns and begin to hate herself, have suicidal ideations, suffer from depression, etc.

A child being bullied at school could start listening to thoughts about self-hatred, rejection, anger, etc. The trauma of being bullied and the negative thought patterns could eventually manifest as a mental illness and / or behavioral issues.

The point of these examples is to help you see that many mental health cases could be linked to some sort of past or present sin, trauma, lifestyle pattern and / or believe system.

What about you? Did you go through trauma in your childhood? How has your life gone so far? Do you have any false belief systems?

I'm in the Flames of Hell

When I worked in the behavioral health field, I met a woman in her early 40's who was struggling with a mental illness. This lady reported to me that she had three kids living with her ex-husband. She said that he used to beat her and verbally abuse her every day. She told me that she was a normal teenager and at the age of 19 she began using marijuana at parties. Later, she met her husband and had three children.

Within several years of living a life of verbal and physical abuse from her husband, she started hallucinating and was diagnosed mentally ill. I don't know exactly what she was diagnosed with, but I believe she was struggling with schizophrenia.

This is the interesting part; the lady would sit in groups / classes and complain of an excruciating pain underneath her skin. She said her skin always burned.

When I talked to her about the pain she said that God had sent her to hell and even though she lived on earth she was in a spiritual hell. The pain of the hell fire was underneath her skin, she said it seemed as hot as real fire. She said that it hurt so bad. She said that she had lost hope because no doctor could diagnose the pain issue and people thought she was making up the story.

I could see in her eyes that she was being honest with me. She believed what she was experiencing was 100% real. She could feel it in her body. This horrible feeling had lasted for many years and she couldn't get away from it. It had led her to sheer hopelessness to where she thought about suicide almost every day. She could never get any relief from the torment.

You might not be dealing with the same type of symptoms this lady had, but maybe you're dealing with something similar? I want you to know there is great hope for you. Don't lose heart.

One day, I was conversing with the lady and it led to discussing Christianity. I asked about her spiritual life. She said that she was saved (surrendered her life to Jesus) as a young girl and still had faith. She mentioned that she had been prayed over by many people, but still couldn't seem to be free from the flames of hell underneath her skin. She said that she believed Jesus didn't hear her prayers anymore because she was evil and had lost her salvation.

I talked with her and tried to explain the truth that she didn't lose her salvation because God loved her and forgave her. I did my best to show compassion and gently lead her to the truth.

And from Jesus Christ, the faithful witness, the firstborn from the dead, and the ruler over the kings of the earth. To Him who loved us and washed us from our sins in His own blood. -Revelation 1:5

Soon after that conversation I never saw her again at the facility. I hope God someday delivers her from the lies and the torment that she reported to me. It broke my heart to see this woman tormented like she was. I believe there are many people around the world who are being tormented just like that lady was. I pray for them.

Do you see how the woman's mental illness could have possibly been caused by spiritual strongholds built on lies? Do you see how through her own past party lifestyle and the abuse from her husband, strongholds could have attached to her brain and began to change her thought patterns? Could it be that through her own lifestyle choices and her husband's sins against her, the woman was now being tormented?

What I have found is that after the lies get into the mind of an individual, they torment the person with more and more lies. The stronghold keeps the person deceived and tormented through lies, false emotions, and even hallucinations.

If the person keeps believing the lies and negative emotions, they could eventually start seeing things others don't, hearing voices inside their mind, feeling bugs inside of them, living in constant paranoia, being in flames of hell, etc. I truly believe many of these things could be caused by spiritual strongholds built inside a person's soul.

What about you? Do you believe that some mental illness symptoms could possibly be caused by wrong belief systems / spiritual strongholds?

THINGS THAT HELPED ME

Let's say that you believe strongholds are really what's causing the issues you are dealing with. How can you be set free? Well, I can't tell you exactly what to do because I don't know everything about you, how your brain works, how your emotions function, your belief systems, etc. Only Father God truly knows everything about you. He is the one that created you. And the good news is, you are very special to Him.

In the Bible you can see that Jesus had different ways of how He healed people. You can't put the Creator in a box. In my own Christian ministry, I have seen some people receive instant miracles and others like myself, walk out their healing over a period of time.

I do not understand why the difference, but I choose to continue to trust God's word no matter what it may look like. Everybody is different, and God chooses to heal us how He wants to. Our job is to continue to believe His truth until we see the promise of healing come to pass in our lives.

I do want to offer you some simple things that I used to help grow in my relationship with God, receive more of His love, and to walk out my healing. As I did these things and continued to surrender my life to Jesus, I started to walk freer and freer from the torment of mental illness.

Becoming a Disciple of Jesus Christ

Then He said to them all, "If anyone desires to come after Me, let him deny himself, and take up his cross daily, and follow Me. -Luke 9:23

That was my first step. I truly decided in my heart to become a disciple of Jesus Christ. Not a religious person, but to passionately pursue a personal relationship with God. I chose to read Jesus' words, believe what He said, and do them. It wasn't always easy, but I did (and still do) my best to put Jesus first in my life and circumstances.

If you haven't been born again or what is referred to as saved and would like to start a personal relationship with Jesus Christ, you can say the prayer below. I believe if you really want to commit your life to Jesus, you can pray, and God's Spirit will meet you right here.

Sample Prayer

"Dear God, I come to You today and choose to confess that I am a sinner that needs You to save me. I ask that You come today and touch my heart and change me. I confess with my mouth Jesus Christ is Lord and believe in my heart that God raised Him from the dead. I ask that You, Jesus, wash away all my sins in Your precious blood and fill me with your Holy Spirit. I choose to become your disciple today. I pray this from my heart to God the Father in the name of Jesus Christ of Nazareth, amen."

If you truly believe you were just saved, congratulations!

As I daily surrendered my heart to Jesus, I learned how to pray. That was one of my number one tools that I learned how to use – prayer. After some time passed from being in the cult in Arkansas, I was less fearful of going to church. I prayed and asked Jesus for a good church and He led me to a Spirit-filled place by my mother's home.

I also learned to worship God. I recommend anyone struggling with mental illness to find time to worship so you can feel the presence of the Holy Spirit and be healed inside and out.

As I attended church regularly, I was invited to prayer meetings. Prayer to me was my life line to God. I couldn't go a day without praying. At first, I started praying for only one minute per night because of the torment and voices in my mind. Yes, I started out small with my prayer life, but eventually could spend one to two hours in prayer. Through the discipline of prayer, I grew closer to Jesus and then one day He showed up for me in a huge way – deliverance!

Realizing Your Authority

When I was dealing with mental health issues, my mother called all the churches in our area and asked for help with her schizophrenic son. Most of the churches said they didn't know how to help me and that I should just continue to receive care from my mental health clinic. I pray for more churches to be equipped to help people suffering with mental illness.

As I began to learn about my spiritual authority as a believer and understand that I could overcome the strongholds, I was ecstatic.

My first introduction to deliverance from strongholds came from receiving a book from a lady that I knew at my local church. I also read over some Christian websites and talked to a couple mature believers about the subject.

I couldn't believe it, for the first time in my life I believed I could be free from the torment. I could break agreements with the lies and command any evil spirit that somehow could be attached to my mind to go in Jesus' name. What a revelation, what a miracle, what hope I had!

So, one day, I began to pray as I walked around my mother's pool out back of her house. I was walking back and forth, round and round, praying to Jesus and asking Him to help me cast out the voices.

With my new found spiritual authority I started to renounce the lies and command the voices and evil spirits to leave me in the name of Jesus. After about one hour of praying and commanding, I felt a huge spiritual force fly out of my head. It left with so much force that I fell to the ground. I was so happy! I laid on the pool deck and cried and cried in thankfulness. With that initial deliverance experience I knew that I was on my way to total freedom.

I know this all might be new to you and might sound a little crazy, but it's my own personal experience. I share it to try to help people.

Repentance / Mind Change

Another tool that went along with my prayer life and realizing my authority was repentance. I didn't really understand repentance at the time, but now looking back, that's what I was pretty much doing all along. I call it dealing with the junk. That's what I believe everyone should do – deal with the junk.

What type of junk do you have in your life? Do you still live a lifestyle that is against God's word? What things to you make a practice of doing that is against the command to walk in purity, love and grace?

Beloved, I beg you as sojourners and pilgrims, abstain from fleshly lusts which war against the soul. -1Peter 2:11

My main focus used to be on the junk in my life and how horrible I felt about it all. This made me feel condemned and miserable about myself as a Christian. I would condemn myself over and over again for my missteps. Over time, as I matured, I learned it's best to not focus solely on the junk, but to focus on who lives inside of you. If your main focus is always on the negative, it's hard to not feel condemned all the time.

There is therefore now no condemnation to those who are in Christ Jesus, who do not walk according to the flesh, but according to the Spirit. –Romans 8:1

Set your mind on things above, not on things on the earth. – Colossians 3:2

I believe a Christian should stay focused on the Spirit that indwells them, which is the Spirit of love. As they learn to walk in the Spirit, as the Bible encourages us to, the junk in our character and lives will begin to be removed supernaturally by the Holy Spirit in us. Our job as followers of Christ is to partner with Him and surrender wholeheartedly to His Lordship. As we learn our identity, and God's will for our life, we start to transform from the inside out.

I say then: walk in the Spirit, and you shall not fulfill the lust of the flesh. -Galatians 5:16

Love does no harm to a neighbor; therefore love is the fulfillment of the law. -Romans 13:10

Therefore be imitators of God as dear children. And walk in love, as Christ also has loved us and given Himself for us, an offering and a sacrifice to God for a sweet-smelling aroma. -Ephesians 5:1:2

Walking in fellowship with Jesus involves renewing our minds, learning to love, and deciding to make better life choices.

Repentance means to change your mind. When you change your mind, your behavior will start changing as well.

If you begin to make an effort to stop believing lies, you can start receiving more spiritual freedom. If you continuing to agree with lies and to listen to voices in your mind, as well as not treating yourself and others with love, it could be harder to get the strongholds to leave. You could be what the Bible calls living in the flesh.

Now the works of the flesh are evident, which are: adultery, fornication, uncleanness, lewdness, idolatry, sorcery, hatred, contentions, jealousies, outbursts of wrath, selfish ambitions, dissensions, heresies, envy, murders, drunkenness, revelries, and the like; of which I tell you beforehand, just as I also told you in time past, that those who practice such things will not inherit the kingdom of God. -Galatians 5:19-21

If this is the case, ask the Lord to help you repent – to change your mind. As I said before, when you start to believe right, you will supernaturally begin to change by the Holy Spirit. I believe that walking in the Spirit is to walk in love.

The transformation process takes time. Be patient and give yourself lots of grace. As the saying goes - Rome wasn't built in a day.

If walking in the flesh describes a loved one, don't be discouraged. Continue to pray and trust your loving Heavenly Father to get a hold of their heart. God loves the people you care about more than you do.

When I first started to change my mind, I asked the Lord about the things in my life that I should let go of. I prayed and studied His word to find His will. I changed my mind about partaking of sexual sin, did my best to stop arguing with people, worked on letting go of unforgiveness I was holding on to towards others, and some other personal things. I also changed my mind about having conversations with and believing anything the voices in my mind were saying.

I can't recommend more the importance of living a lifestyle of repentance – mind change.

And Jesus answered and said to them, "Do you suppose that these Galileans were worse sinners than all other Galileans, because they suffered such things? I tell you, no; but unless you repent you will all likewise perish. -Luke 13:2-3

I am thankful for the grace God gave me to be free from many things. Yes, to this day, I still live a lifestyle of repentance and always will. For me, it's part of my walk with Jesus. God wants to transform us, and He can do so when we agree and align our ourselves with His word.

For as many as are led by the Spirit of God, these are sons of God. -Romans 8:14

But if you are led by the Spirit, you are not under the law. -Galatians 5:18

I personally believe that on this side of eternity you will always be going through some sort of transformation process. He wants to live His life through you, and that to me seems like a whole lot of transformation, doesn't it?

Worship

Becoming a worshipper helped me immensely. I learned how to worship from my heart. I would go to worship concerts and many different church services to get in to God's presence and be healed. When you worship the Lord, His presence comes, and in His presence is fullness of joy, healing, deliverance and freedom.

Now the Lord is the Spirit; and where the Spirit of the Lord is, there is liberty. -2Corinthians 3:17

One of the smartest things that I can remember doing that helped me with my worship and prayer life was purchasing a MP3 player and downloading some good Spirit-filled worship music. You can find good worship music online if you search for it. I would put in my earphones and turn up the music or the audio Bible and go on long walks while I prayed and worshipped God.

I can't tell you how much this helped me. I highly recommend it. The music in the earphones helped drown out the voices and at the same time helped me focus more on my Savior. It worked great. Maybe you should try it?

Fighting the Good Fight

The foundational things I learned, reading the word, prayer, worship, repentance, etc., helped me at my next step – fighting the good fight. I decided in my heart that I was going to drive out every lie and every spiritual stronghold from my soul no matter how long it took. I was determined to not give up until I saw victory.

Almost every day I would put on my earphones, pray, worship God, break agreements with the lies and command them to come out / off my mind in the name of Jesus. Within one year's time I was completely set free from the torment of schizophrenia.

You might say, "One year? That's too long!" and my reply is, "It took me one year, it could take you only one day, one week, one month, or longer. It doesn't matter how long it takes because freedom is well worth it, isn't it?"

If you have decided to become a disciple of Jesus and want to gain victory over the strongholds, then I believe your attitude should be someone who is in it for the long haul.

Are you willing to keep moving forward in Jesus? I was willing and guess what? God came through for me. I am free and even have a Letter of Decertification to prove it!

The type of heart attitude I had was this – I told God if I was never healed of schizophrenia, I would still do my best to follow Him. Is this you today? Are you willing to still follow Jesus if for some reason you never receive your healing?

If you have a hard time with having this type of heart attitude, ask Father God to help you get there. He is faithful to answer your sincere prayers.

Have I not commanded you? Be strong and of good courage; do not be afraid, nor be dismayed, for the Lord your God is with you wherever you go. -Joshua 1:9

"Ask, and it will be given to you; seek, and you will find; knock, and it will be opened to you. For everyone w`ho asks receives, and he who seeks finds, and to him who knocks it will be opened. -Matthew 7:7-8

Mentorship

Being mentored by a mature Christian could help you tremendously. I have found that the thoughts and / or voices tormenting an individual try to get the person to isolate. They do not want the person to go to a healthy church, prayer meetings, Bible studies, or to fellowship with other Christians.

Don't listen to the lies anymore. Do your best to get out of bed, walk out of your house, and maybe if you feel led to, go to a church service or prayer meeting.

If you are still struggling to get out of your house, that's okay, I recommend trying to find some good teachings to listen to or watch on television and / or the Internet. Try to find someone who preaches the message of grace, truth and love. I have found that many times the spiritual strongholds try to pull people, who may already struggle with fear, to listen to condemning teachings focused on self-righteousness, legalism, and hell. Fear can be used as a weapon to try to torment you.

Inasmuch then as the children have partaken of flesh and blood, He Himself likewise shared in the same, that through death He might destroy him who had the power of death, that is, the devil, and release those who through fear of death were all their lifetime subject to bondage. -Hebrews 14:15

He who does not love does not know God, for God is love. -1John 4:8

God is not mad at you and in fact wants you to intimately know Him as your best friend. Don't take my word for it, but instead believe what God's word says. If you believe in Jesus, then you are like Abraham. You are called a friend of God!

And the Scripture was fulfilled which says, "Abraham believed God, and it was accounted to him for righteousness." And he was called the friend of God. -James 2:23

One day at church, I met a Christian counselor. This counselor helped me through a lot of the deliverance process that I went through. I am very thankful to God for sending me a counselor when He did.

Sometimes my thoughts got very negative and my counselor / mentor would help me see things in a different light. Through counseling and the word of God, I learned many truths that helped set me free from lies. Without being mentored it would have been a lot harder for me.

I believe you need to find a good Christian mentor who can relate to, pray for, and encourage you. Would you please pray and ask Jesus to send someone to help you? I honestly prayed for a long while until my first mentor showed up. God always answers prayers, but not usually in our timing. Be patient, He will answer in His perfect timing. I believe having some sort of mentor is vital to spiritual accountability and growth.

Never Give Up

I want to encourage you to not worry about taking medications. Father God is not mad at you for taking psyche meds. It's not a sin to take medications to help you with symptoms. Taking medications or getting medical treatment is nowhere listed in the Bible as sin.

Think of it this way, it's not a sin to put a bandage over your wound, is it? The same way you can use a bandage to cover a wound is the same way you can take medications to cover a symptom of a mental illness or any other sickness.

If you have thoughts / voices condemning you for taking prescribed medications it's time for you to break that lie. Don't believe lies anymore, instead tell the lying thoughts to be quiet and come out / off your mind in the name of Jesus.

The voices used to tell me that my medications were evil and if I took them then it meant that I had no faith. It was all a big lie, based in fear. I don't (and can't) give medical advice, but one thing I can tell you is always take your meds as prescribed. Many times, I would skip days or weeks and that really messed with the chemicals in my brain. It made my mind seem even more tormented at times. Please remember to always take your medications as prescribed by a licensed medical doctor.

After growing in faith and in my personal relationship with Jesus, I started to feel better. I worked with my family, clinical team, and psychiatrist to wean off the medications slowly. It took a while, but I eventually weaned off all of them.

Please know that you're not a failure if you take medications and Father God is not mad at you at all. He understands what you are dealing with and if it is your desire to eventually wean off the meds, let your doctors and supporters know. You may be surprised with who wants to help you achieve your recovery goals.

And if weening off your meds is not a goal, that's perfectly fine. Know that Jesus loves you if you are on medications or not. It makes no difference to Him. He loves you because you're His child.

Another thing that helped me was every time the voices came and told me I was evil or that I had no faith for taking meds, I prayed from my heart to God. I told Him that I was taking the meds for the symptoms of mental illness but was looking towards Him as my healer.

Guess what? It eventually started working. The voices of condemnation and guilt left me. Maybe give that a try if the voices make you feel bad for taking meds. All the voices ever did to me was lie, lie, and lie some more.

I'm glad I covered the medication issues that tormented me for so long. I hope what I wrote here helps someone dealing with a similar issue. Once again, God loves you the exact same if you take medications or not. Believe it!

Along with repentance and learning how to worship and pray, you can minister deliverance to yourself. It's actually quite simple to do. I am sharing what helped me. Maybe it will help you too?

Try to find a quiet place like a bedroom or living room. Lie down on a bed, comfy chair, or couch. Close your eyes and start to pray to Jesus and confess your favorite scriptures and ask Him to wash you in His precious blood. Ask Him to come by His Spirit and to help you receive freedom. Thank Him for His love, mercy and grace. Thank Him for His compassion on your life and for the wonderful future He has planned for you. Thank God for the authority of Jesus that dwells in you by the Holy Spirit.

When you are ready, take a couple of deep breaths and then say something similar to the below prayer.

Father God, I thank you that the Bible says I have been translated from the power of darkness to the Kingdom of Light and no weapon formed against me can ever prosper. I choose to renounce and break agreements with every lie that I may have been believing. I also renounce all negative lying emotions that do not line up with your truth. The truth is, I am forgiven and have the Holy Spirit in me and am a beloved child of God. I now command all lies and feelings that are not from God to disconnect from me now, in Jesus' name. I thank You God for the power I have in You to drive out / off evil spirits. In the name of Jesus Christ of Nazareth, I speak to every spiritual stronghold, I break agreement with you and command you all to come out / off me right now. In the name of Jesus Christ, come out / off now!

You can keep saying this type of prayer until you may feel things loosing your mind and body. You can lay hands on yourself and command anything that's not from God to leave in Jesus' name. You have all authority through your faith in Jesus.

Behold, I give you the authority to trample on serpents and scorpions, and over all the power of the enemy, and nothing shall by any means hurt you. Nevertheless do not rejoice in this, that the spirits are subject to you, but rather rejoice because your names are written in heaven." -Luke *10:19-20*

In my years of ministry, I have witnessed evil spirits come out / off people through different ways. Sometimes the person has no outward manifestation, they just say they feel a lot lighter after prayer. Sometimes the person coughs, yawns, or even feels a need to spit during prayer. I know it may sound a bit weird and maybe a little crazy, but this is what I have personally experienced.

Yes, it did take me some time and perseverance to start feeling better but that was okay with me. I was so thankful to find some relief from the voices and torment. If nothing happens when you start out, that's okay, don't be discouraged. Father God has a plan specifically designed for you. Continue walking with Jesus.

You can also do the aforementioned prayers (commonly referred to as self-deliverance) during your private times with the Lord whenever you feel led to. Remember that your ultimate goal is to personally know Jesus and to not spend every prayer time doing self-deliverance.

I recommend only doing self-deliverance when prompted to do so by the Holy Spirit. You want your main focus to be on fellowshipping with God and not on strongholds. Focus on God and He can work all things out for your good.

A couple of things I found that really help is to have a soft heart towards Jesus, and to do your best to not have any conversations with thoughts / voices in your mind.

I believe if you continue with Jesus and renew your mind with His truth the strongholds can be removed. Remember that walking with Jesus is a life long journey. Give yourself lots of love, mercy and grace along the way. And don't put too much pressure on yourself to be perfect in your flesh. Instead, rely on the Holy Spirit inside of you to transform you from glory to glory. Learn His ways, what He likes, and what He dislikes. Stay of a humble heart and do your best to forgive others and to love your neighbor as yourself.

But we all, with unveiled face, beholding as in a mirror the glory of the Lord, are being transformed into the same image from glory to glory, just as by the Spirit of the Lord. -2Corinthians 3:18

Owe no one anything except to love one another, for he who loves another has fulfilled the law. -Romans 13:8

Please remember that a Christian dealing with a mental illness does not mean they are a bad person, lost, or not on their way to heaven. They are just as saved as every other believer. This is because we are all saved (and remain saved) by grace and not by our own works. God is faithful to never leave or forsake you.

Even when we were dead in sins, hath quickened us together with Christ, (by grace ye are saved;) -Ephesians 2:5

And I give them eternal life, and they shall never perish; neither shall anyone snatch them out of My hand. My Father, who has given them to Me, is greater than all; and no one is able to snatch them out of My Father's hand. I and My Father are one." -John 10:28-30

I used to worry that I lost my salvation because I was dealing with the voices and lies. If this is you, please stop worrying, If Jesus is your Savior than you are in His hand. God is so kind and good, He is your Heavenly Father. No need for you to worry anymore.

If you have been believing a lie that you may have lost your salvation, you're not alone. This is a huge lie that many, many Christians fall for. Renounce that lie and move forward today. Your salvation is eternal. Be encouraged that the Holy Spirit is with you always and forever.

Now He who has prepared us for this very thing is God, who also has given us the Spirit as a guarantee. -2Corithians 5:5

Let your conduct be without covetousness; be content with such things as you have. For He Himself has said, "I will never leave you nor forsake you." -Hebrews 13:5

DEFEATING THE LIES

I believe one major reason people with mental illness sometimes take a while to gain freedom is because of conditioning of the mind to believe lies over and over again.

In my own walk, I noticed sometimes it took me a while to overcome a specific lie or negative emotion. For instance, I used to operate heavily in a mindset and emotion of rejection. I had a belief that everyone hated me. It was hard to overcome because the belief came with a strong negative emotion. I battled that stronghold for a long period of time. It negatively affected my job, family, and personal relationships. But with walking through that battle with the Lord's help, I gained many valuable insights to help others overcome rejection.

Good news is, now, if I am dealing with something negative in my life, I understand that it will eventually work out for my good, just like the Bible promises. Gaining this revelation from God's word has made it easier for me to walk through life's ups and downs.

And not only that, but we also glory in tribulations, knowing that tribulation produces perseverance; and perseverance, character; and character, hope. -Romans 5:3:4

And we know that all things work together for good to those who love God, to those who are the called according to His purpose. -Romans 8:28

An exercise that helped me was I would write down every lie that I was believing about myself, my life situations, other people, and God. For instance, I wrote down things like "I'm going to hell" or "I'm ugly" or "I will never be married". I wrote down all the lies. After I wrote them down, then I went through the Bible and found all the scriptures that defeated those particular lies. The word of God is a sharp sword to defeat the deception.

For the word of God is living and powerful, and sharper than any two-edged sword, piercing even to the division of soul and spirit, and of joints and marrow, and is a discerner of the thoughts and intents of the heart. -Hebrews 4:12

After finding a verse or two that dealt with a specific lie, I then would renounce the lie and speak the truth from what I found in the Bible. I would do that exercise daily until the lies were eventually destroyed. I believe this is a major tool to pull down a stronghold, keep beating it with truth until it crumbles.

For some people, it may take longer than others to defeat certain lies because some lies have been ingrained in us since childhood. For instance, a person believes a lie their mother told them when they were five years old. They have lived with that lie ingrained inside their mind for 50+ years. Do you see how it could take this person a little longer to defeat the lie from childhood? God is faithful to help you no matter how ingrained a lie has been inside of you.

It seems to me that spiritual strongholds are formed by thoughts being thrown at the mind like an arrow into someone's head. If one of the arrows (lies) gets into the person's mind and they receive it as truth, then a couple more arrows (lies) get thrown at them. If they receive those, the arrows just keep coming. A stronghold is eventually built.

A key that I find helps, is to recognize when it's a lying thought or a negative emotion being thrown at you. Then, after you recognize it, catch it, renounce it, and kick it out in Jesus' name. Do your best to learn to catch the lies when they first hit your mind. If you don't catch the lie there, it could turn in to a negative emotion. And after the negative emotion manifests, it could lead to you doing something in the flesh you'll most likely regret later.

An example of this; you get a thought that your co-worker doesn't like you. You dwell on the thought and you then start to feel an emotion of rejection and hatred towards your co-worker. You then allow the negative emotions to manifest in your flesh in the form of yelling at your co-worker. You end up getting fired from your job.

Do you see how believing lies can eventually lead someone towards negative behaviors? That's why repentance (mind change) is so important.

Do your best to partner with the Holy Spirit to learn to catch the lies in your mind and to not receive negative emotions. God's word will help you discern what's true and what's false.

For though we walk in the flesh, we do not war according to the flesh. For the weapons of our warfare are not carnal but mighty in God for pulling down strongholds, casting down arguments and every high thing that exalts itself against the knowledge of God, bringing every thought into captivity to the obedience of Christ, and being ready to punish all disobedience when your obedience is fulfilled. -2Corinthians 10:3-6

I hope you move forward to demolish strongholds with truth, learn to catch arrows, and to not receive lies in your soul anymore. It takes some time to learn this discipline but going through the journey will be well worth it in the end. I believe you will learn some great things that will help others overcome as well. I truly believe you are called to become a powerfully anointed friend of God.

For I know the thoughts that I think toward you, says the Lord, thoughts of peace and not of evil, to give you a future and a hope. -Jeremiah 29:11

FINAL WORD

You are not your diagnosis. You are a beloved child of the God that has already been set free 2000+ years ago. I honestly believe mental illness is not incurable as many people say. I am living proof that you can be delivered and healed. Be encouraged that life is not hopeless, and that you have great value to God. Please remember to continue to move forward with Jesus. Never give up because He has a great destiny for you and your family. God bless you!

My Prayer For You

"Father God, I pray for the person reading this, I pray the revelation that they can be set free from mental illness enlightens them. As someone who has personally been delivered of schizophrenia by faith in You, I ask that the same courage, faith, and strength that You gave me be given to this person. I pray the anointing of the Holy Spirit rest upon them as they decide to become a disciple of Jesus, to walk in repentance, to grow in their prayer life, to worship Jesus, to operate in faith and love, and to renounce and let go of every lie in Jesus' name. Help this person to never give up, but to pursue You fervently. I ask that You find them a good Christian mentor, someone who will help them through this time in their life. Most of all, I pray they grow extremely close to the Holy Spirit. Please remind them every day that they are not alone, but that You are

their shield, defender, refuge, healer and deliverer. Thank you for loving the mentally ill, Lord Jesus, amen."

Some Scriptures to Help You

In this is love, not that we loved God, but that He loved us and sent His Son to be the propitiation for our sins. -1John 4:10

"I, even I, am He who blots out your transgressions for My own sake; And I will not remember your sins. -Isaiah 43:25

And it shall come to pass that whoever calls on the name of the Lord shall be saved. For in Mount Zion and in Jerusalem there shall be deliverance, as the Lord has said, among the remnant whom the Lord calls. -Joel 2:32

Then Peter said to them, "Repent, and let every one of you be baptized in the name of Jesus Christ for the remission of sins; and you shall receive the gift of the Holy Spirit. -Acts 2:38

For whatever is born of God overcomes the world. And this is the victory that has overcome the world— your faith. Who is he who overcomes the world, but he who believes that Jesus is the Son of God? -1John 5:4-5

Call upon Me in the day of trouble; I will deliver you, and you shall glorify Me. -Psalm 50:15

You are my hiding place; You shall preserve me from trouble; You shall surround me with songs of deliverance. Selah. -Psalm 32:7

He has delivered us from the power of darkness and conveyed us into the kingdom of the Son of His love, in whom we have redemption through His blood, the forgiveness of sins. -Colossians 1:13-14

No weapon formed against you shall prosper, and every tongue which rises against you in judgment you shall condemn. This is the heritage of the servants of the Lord, and their righteousness is from Me," says the Lord. -Isaiah 54:17

Is anyone among you suffering? Let him pray. Is anyone cheerful? Let him sing psalms. Is anyone among you sick? Let him call for the elders of the church, and let them pray over him, anointing him with oil in the name of the Lord. And the prayer of faith will save the sick, and the Lord will raise him up. And if he has committed sins, he will be forgiven. Confess your trespasses to one another, and pray for one another, that you may be healed. The effective, fervent prayer of a righteous man avails much. -James 5:13-16

But He was wounded for our transgressions, He was bruised for our iniquities; the chastisement for our peace was upon Him, and by His stripes we are healed. -Isaiah 53:5

And he said: "The Lord is my rock and my fortress and my deliverer; the God of my strength, in whom I will trust; my shield and the horn of my salvation, my stronghold and my refuge; my Savior, You save me from violence. -2Samuel 22:2-3

Blessed is the man to whom the Lord shall not impute sin. -Romans 4:8

For God has not given us a spirit of fear, but of power and of love and of a sound mind. -2Timothy 1:7

And you will seek Me and find Me, when you search for Me with all your heart. -Jeremiah 29:13

He has not dealt with us according to our sins, nor punished us according to our iniquities. For as the heavens are high above the earth, so great is

His mercy toward those who fear Him; as far as the east is from the west, so far has He removed our transgressions from us. -Psalm 103:10-12

For by one offering He has perfected forever those who are being sanctified. -Hebrews 10:14

The Lord is gracious and full of compassion, Slow to anger and great in mercy. The Lord is good to all, and His tender mercies are over all His works. -Psalm 145:8-9

Bless the Lord, O my soul; and all that is within me, bless His holy name! Bless the Lord, O my soul, and forget not all His benefits: who forgives all your iniquities, who heals all your diseases, who redeems your life from destruction, who crowns you with lovingkindness and tender mercies, who satisfies your mouth with good things, so that your youth is renewed like the eagle's. -Psalm 103:1-5

Finally, my brethren, be strong in the Lord and in the power of His might. Put on the whole armor of God, that you may be able to stand against the wiles of the devil. For we do not wrestle against flesh and blood, but against principalities, against powers, against the rulers of the darkness of this age, against spiritual hosts of wickedness in the heavenly places. Therefore take up the whole armor of God, that you may be able to withstand in the evil day, and having done all, to stand. Stand therefore, having girded your waist with truth, having put on the breastplate of righteousness, and having shod your feet with the preparation of the gospel of peace; above all, taking the shield of faith with which you will be able to quench all the fiery darts of the wicked one. And take the helmet of salvation, and the sword of the Spirit, which is the word of God; praying always with all prayer and supplication in the Spirit, being watchful to this end with all perseverance and supplication for all the saints. -Ephesians 6:10-18

He heals the brokenhearted and binds up their wounds. -Psalm 147:3

Come to Me, all you who labor and are heavy laden, and I will give you rest. Take My yoke upon you and learn from Me, for I am gentle and lowly in heart, and you will find rest for your souls. For My yoke is easy and My burden is light." -Matthew 11:28-30

Printed in the United States
By Bookmasters